EASY GUITAR WITH NOTES & TAB

best of The Beach Boys

2 STRUM AND PICK PATTERNS
6 Barbara Ann
8 Be True to Your School
3 California Girls
10 409
16 Fun, Fun, Fun
13 God Only Knows
18 Good Vibrations
22 Help Me Rhonda
28 I Get Around
30 In My Room
32 Kokomo
25 Little Deuce Coupe
36 Shut Down
39 Sloop John B
42 Surfer Girl
44 Surfin'
46 Surfin' Safari
52 Surfin' U.S.A.
48 Wouldn't It Be Nice

ISBN 978-0-634-03235-6

HAL•LEONARD® CORPORATION
7777 W. BLUEMOUND RD. P.O. BOX 13819 MILWAUKEE, WI 53213

For all works contained herein:
Unauthorized copying, arranging, adapting, recording or public performance is an infringement of copyright.
Infringers are liable under the law.

Visit Hal Leonard Online at
www.halleonard.com

T0019103

STRUM AND PICK PATTERNS

This chart contains the suggested strum and pick patterns that are referred to by number at the beginning of each song in this book. The symbols ⊓ and v in the strum patterns refer to down and up strokes, respectively. The letters in the pick patterns indicate which right-hand fingers plays which strings.

p = thumb
i = index finger
m = middle finger
a = ring finger

For example; Pick Pattern 2
is played: thumb - index - middle - ring

Strum Patterns

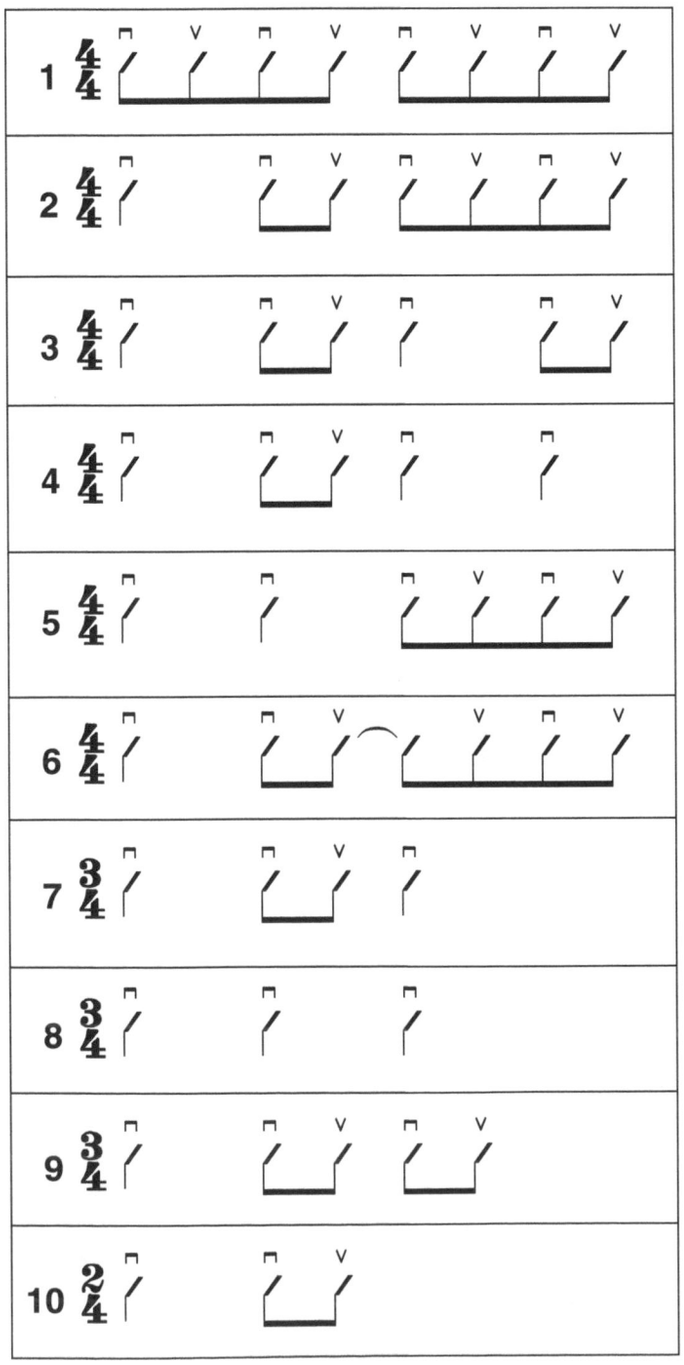

Pick Patterns

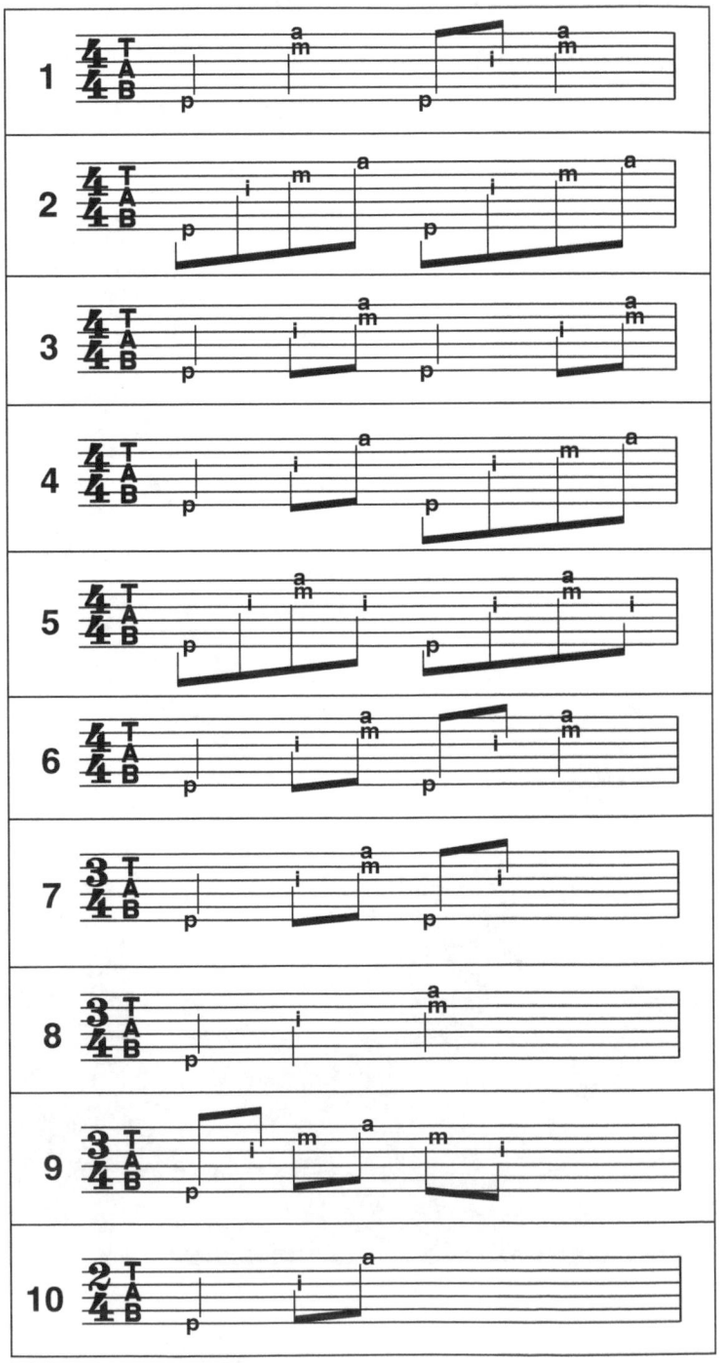

You can use the 3/4 Strum or Pick Patterns in songs written in compound meter (6/8, 9/8, 12/8, etc.). For example, you can accompany a song in 6/8 by playing the 3/4 pattern twice in each measure. The 4/4 Strum and Pick Patterns can be used for songs written in cut time (¢) by doubling the note time values in the patterns. Each pattern would therefore last two measures in cut time.

California Girls

Words and Music by Brian Wilson and Mike Love

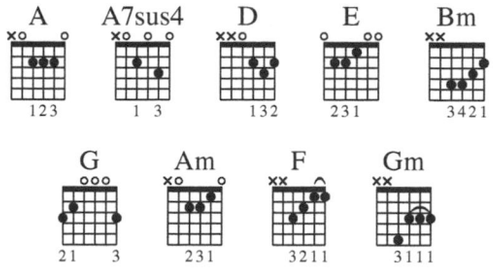

Strum Pattern: 1, 2
Pick Pattern: 2, 4

Intro

Moderately (♩♩ = ♩³♪)

N.C. *Play 4 times* *rit.*

mf

A tempo **Verse**

A A

1. Well, East Coast girls are hip,
2. *See additional lyrics*

A7sus4

I real - ly dig those styles they wear. And the

Copyright © 1965 IRVING MUSIC, INC.
Copyright Renewed
All Rights Reserved Used by Permission

D
E
South - ern girls with the way they talk they knock me out when I'm down there.

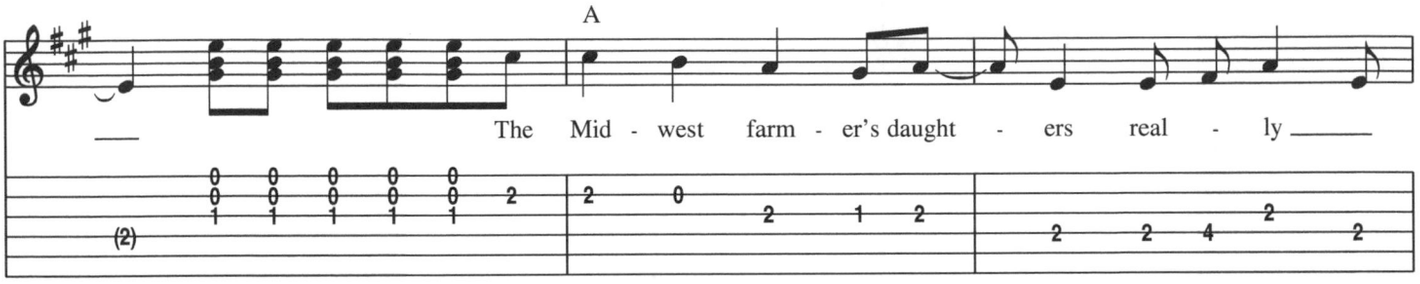
A
The Mid - west farm - er's daught - ers real - ly

A7sus4
D
make you feel al - right. And the North - ern girls with the

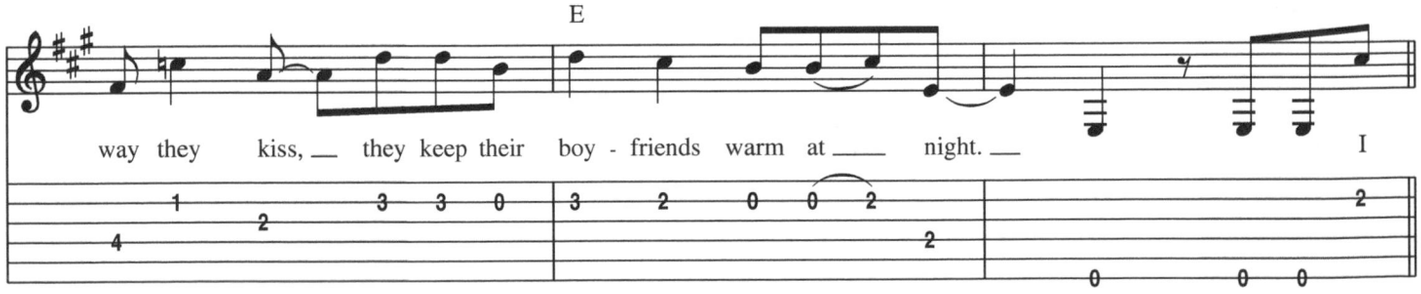
E
way they kiss, they keep their boy - friends warm at night.
I

Chorus
A
Bm
G
wish they all could be Cal - i - for - nia girls. Wish they all could be

Additional Lyrics

2. The West Coast has the sunshine,
And the girls all get so tan.
I dig a French bikini on Hawaiian islands dolls,
By a palm tree in the sand.
I been all around this great big world
And I've seen all kinds of girls.
Yeah, but I couldn't wait to get back in the states,
Back to the cutest girls in the world.

Barbara Ann

Words and Music by Fred Fassert

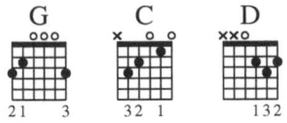

Strum Pattern: 2
Pick Pattern: 4

Intro-Chorus
Bright Rock

N.C. (G)

mf

Ba - Ba - Ba - Ba - Bar - bara Ann. Ba - Ba - Ba - Ba - Ba - Ba - Bar - bara

Chorus

G C G

Ann, take my hand, Bar - bara Ann.

D C

You got me rock - in' and a - roll - in', rock - in' and a reel - in' Bar - bara

© 1959 (Renewed 1987) EMI LONGITUDE MUSIC and COUSINS MUSIC INC.
All Rights Controlled and Administered by EMI LONGITUDE MUSIC
All Rights Reserved International Copyright Secured Used by Permission

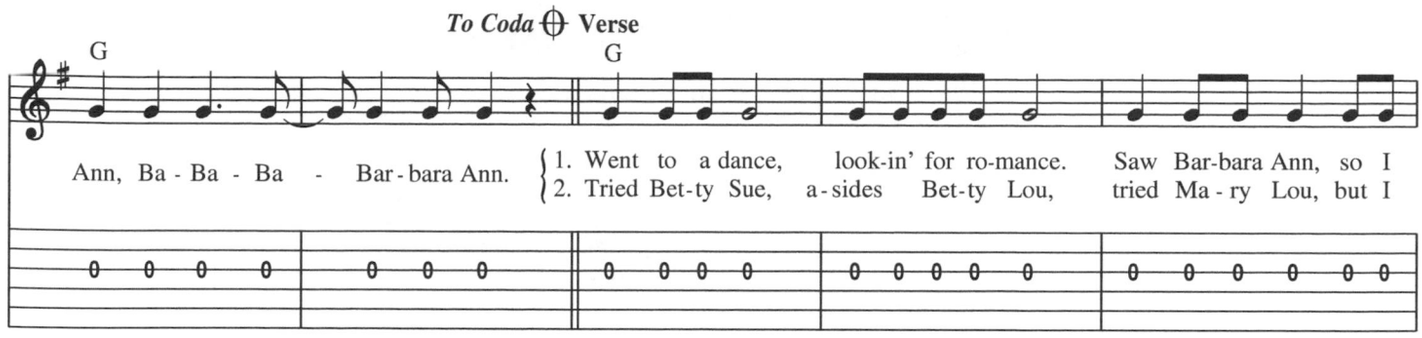
To Coda
Verse
G
G
Ann, Ba - Ba - Ba - Bar - bara Ann.
1. Went to a dance, look-in' for ro-mance. Saw Bar-bara Ann, so I
2. Tried Bet-ty Sue, a-sides Bet-ty Lou, tried Ma - ry Lou, but I

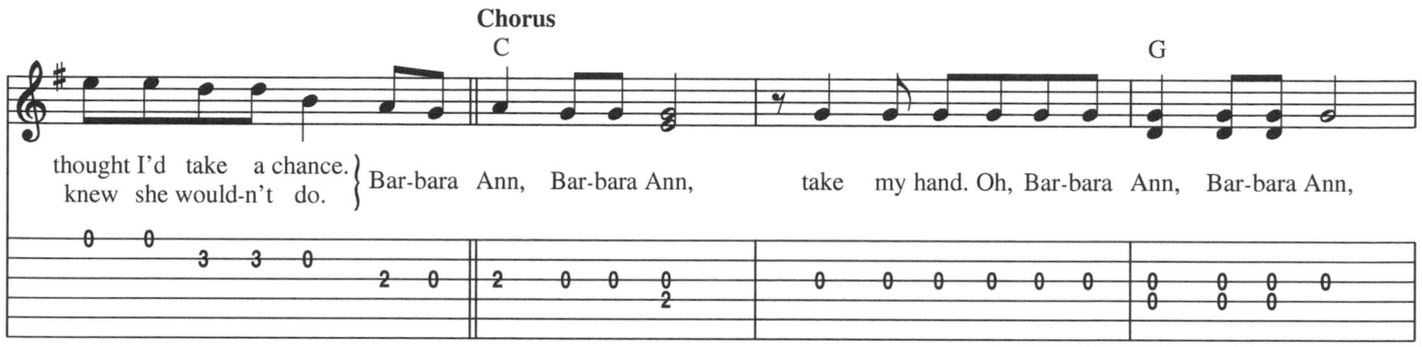
Chorus
C
G
thought I'd take a chance.
knew she would-n't do.
Bar-bara Ann, Bar-bara Ann, take my hand. Oh, Bar-bara Ann, Bar-bara Ann,

D
C
take my hand. You got me rock - in' and a - roll - in', rock - in' and a reel - in' Bar - bara

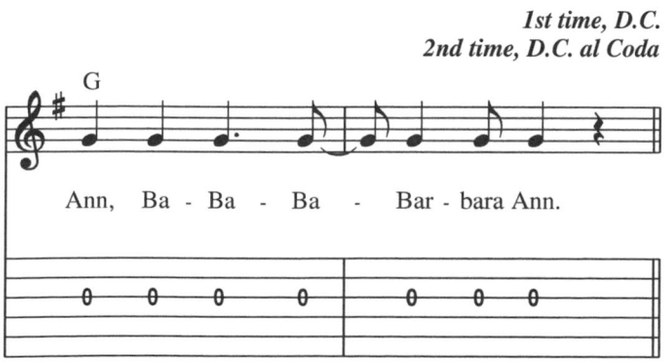
1st time, D.C.
2nd time, D.C. al Coda
G
Ann, Ba - Ba - Ba - Bar - bara Ann.

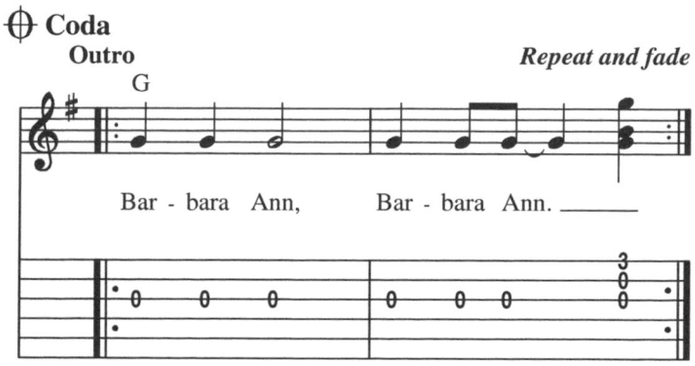
Coda
Outro
Repeat and fade
G
Bar - bara Ann, Bar - bara Ann.

Be True to Your School

Words and Music by Brian Wilson and Mike Love

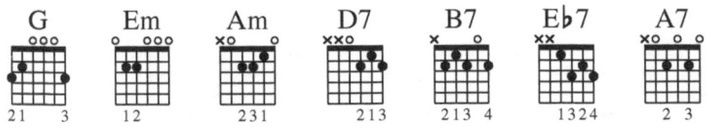

Strum Pattern: 2
Pick Pattern: 4

Verse

Slowly

G Em

mf

1. When some loud brag - gard tries to put me down ___ and says his

2., 3. *See additional lyrics*

Am D7 G

school is great, _ I tell him right a - way, "Now, what's the mat - ter, Bud - dy, ain't you

Em Am D7

heard of my school?_ It's num - ber one in the state." _ So be true to your school, _

Chorus

G B7

_____ just like you would to your girl ____ or guy. _____

Copyright © 1963 IRVING MUSIC, INC.
Copyright Renewed
All Rights Reserved Used by Permission

Additional Lyrics

2. I got a letterman's sweater with the letter in front
   I got for football and track;
   I'm proud to wear it.
   Now, when I cruise around the other parts of town
   I got my decal in back.

3. On Friday we'll be jacked up on the football game
   And I'll be ready to fight.
   We're gonna smash 'em.
   Now, my girl will be workin' on her pom-poms now,
   And she'll be yellin' tonight.

409

Words and Music by Brian Wilson, Gary Usher and Mike Love

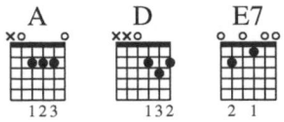

Strum Pattern: 2
Pick Pattern: 4

Intro

Moderately

N.C.(A)

mf

She's real fine, my 4 0 9. ___ She's real fine, my

(E) A

4 0 9, ___ my 4 0 9. ___

Verse

A

___ 1. Well, I saved my pen - nies, and I saved my dimes. _

2. *See additional lyrics*

Copyright © 1962 IRVING MUSIC, INC.
Copyright Renewed
All Rights Reserved Used by Permission

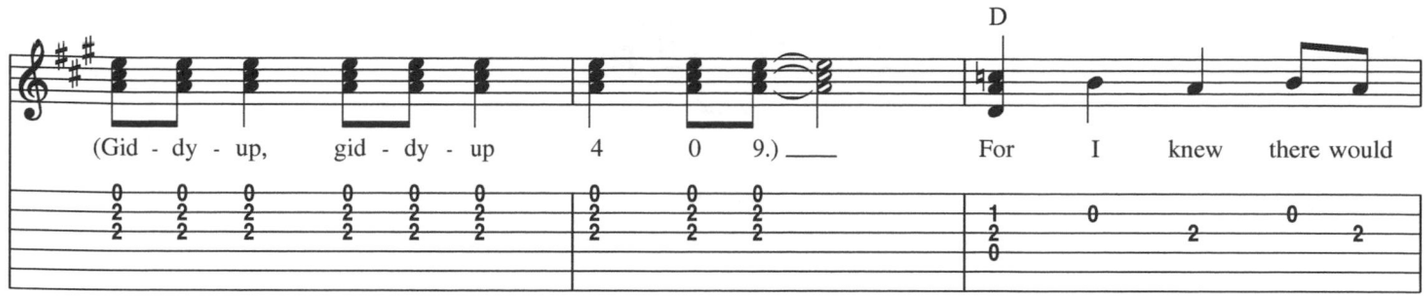
D
(Gid - dy - up, gid - dy - up 4 0 9.) For I knew there would

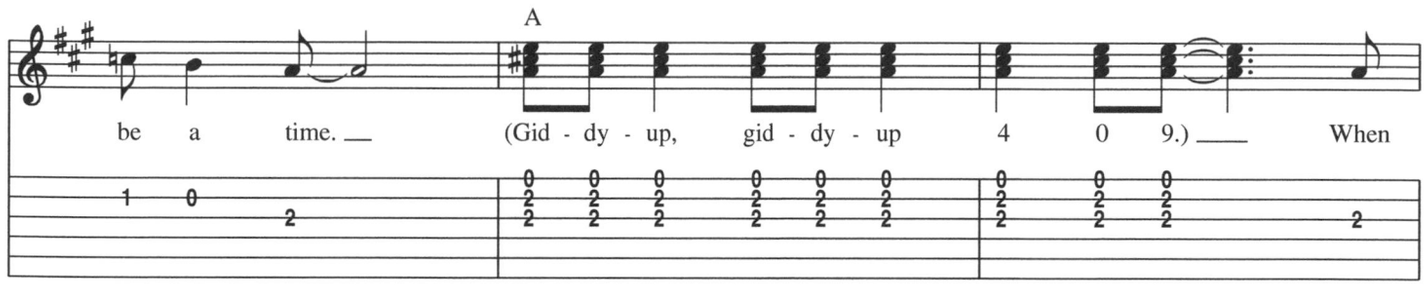
A
be a time. (Gid - dy - up, gid - dy - up 4 0 9.) When

E7
D
A
I would buy a brand new 4 0 9.
(4 0 9.

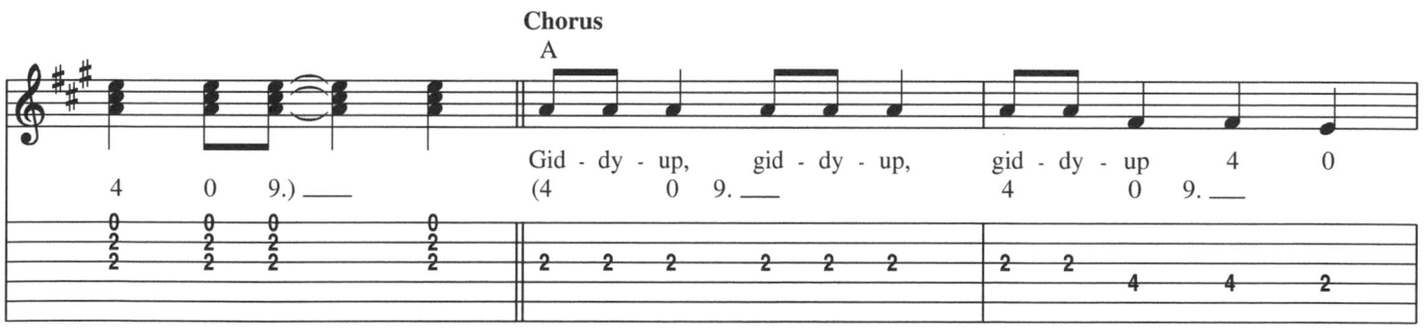
Chorus
A
4 0 9.)
Gid - dy - up, gid - dy - up, gid - dy - up 4 0
(4 0 9.
4 0 9.

D
9. Gid - dy - up, 4 0 9. Gid -
Gid - dy - up, gid - dy - up 4 0 9.
4 0 9.

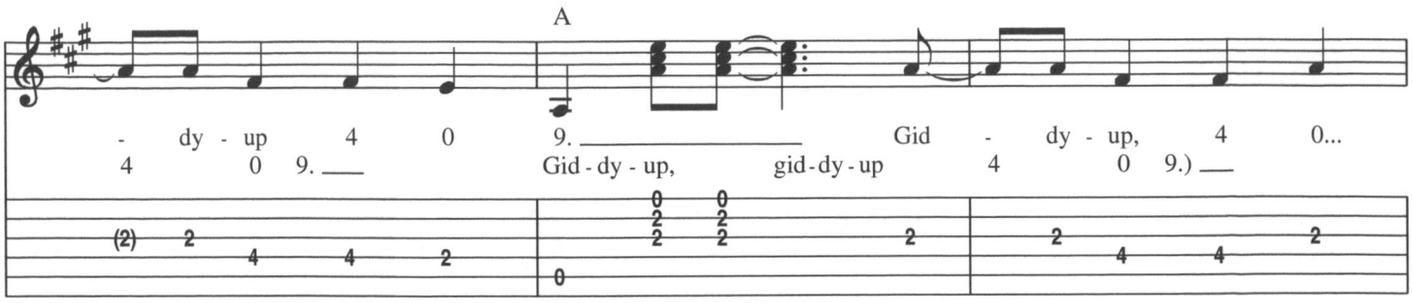

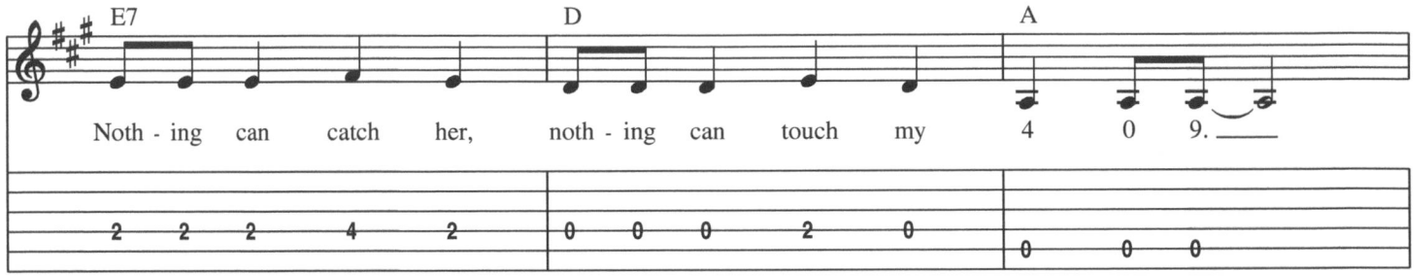

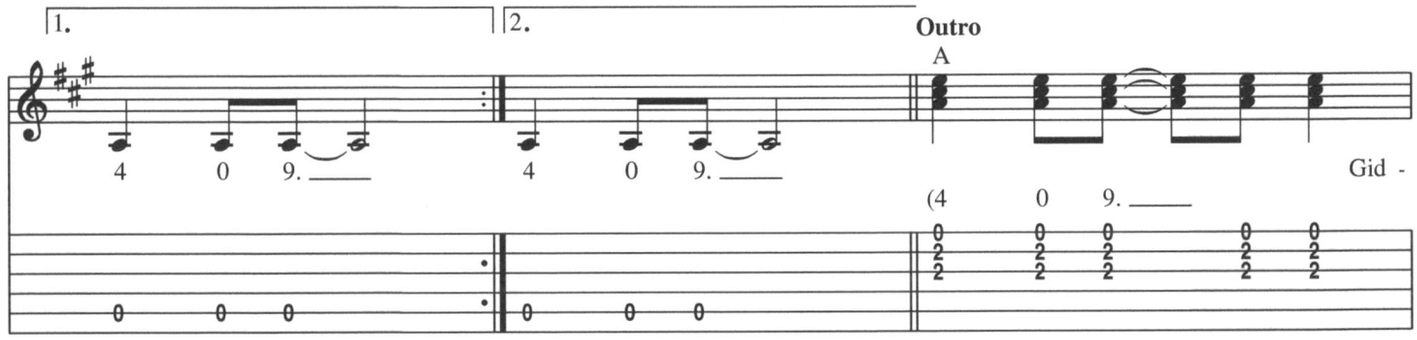

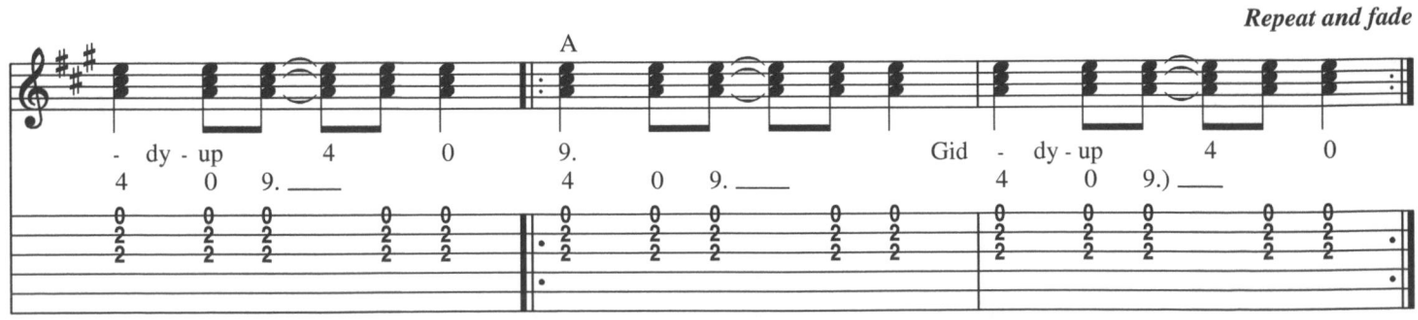

Additional Lyrics

2. When I take her to the drag, she really shines.
(Giddy-up, giddy-up 409.)
She always turns in the fastest time.
(Giddy-up, giddy-up 409.)
My four-speed, dual-quad, posi-traction 409.
(409. 409.)

God Only Knows

Words and Music by Brian Wilson and Tony Asher

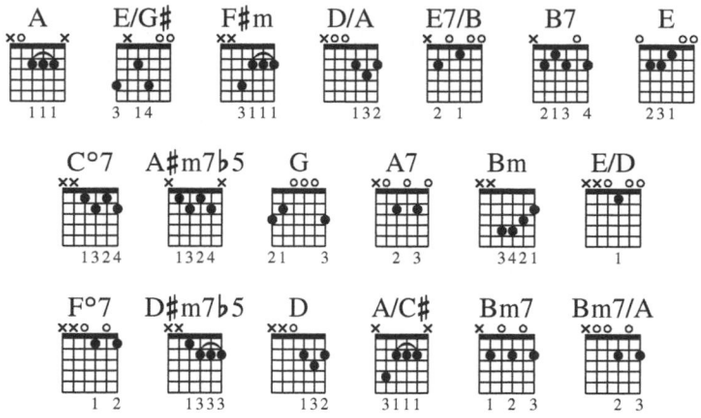

Strum Pattern: 4
Pick Pattern: 3

Intro

Moderately (♩♫ = ♩³♪)

Play 3 times

A E/G♯ F♯m N.C.

mf

Verse

D/A E7/B F♯m B7

1. I may not al - ways love you, but long as there are stars a - bove you,
2. *See additional lyrics*

E C°7 E A♯m7♭5

you nev - er need to doubt it, I'll make you so sure a - bout it.

Copyright © 1966 IRVING MUSIC, INC.
Copyright Renewed
All Rights Reserved Used by Permission

Interlude

Bridge

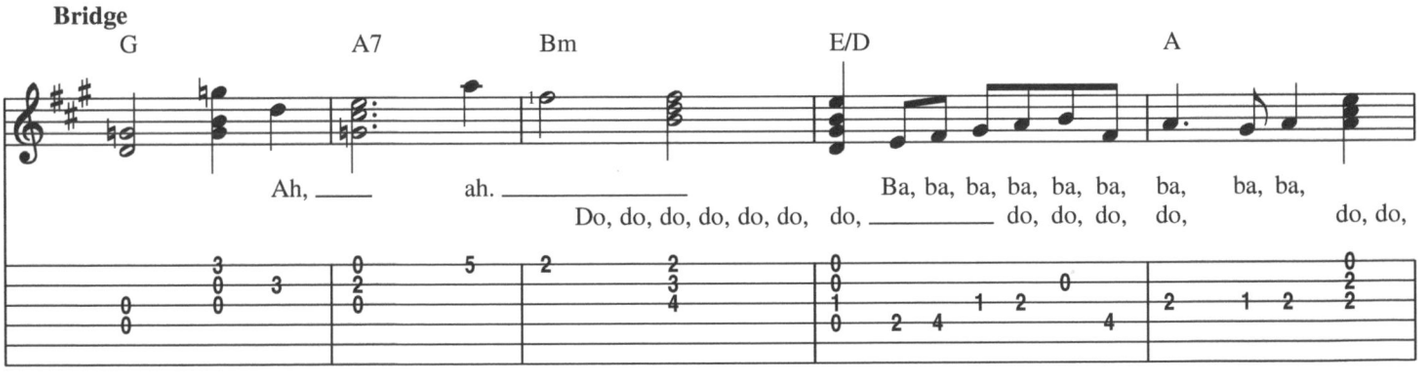

Chorus

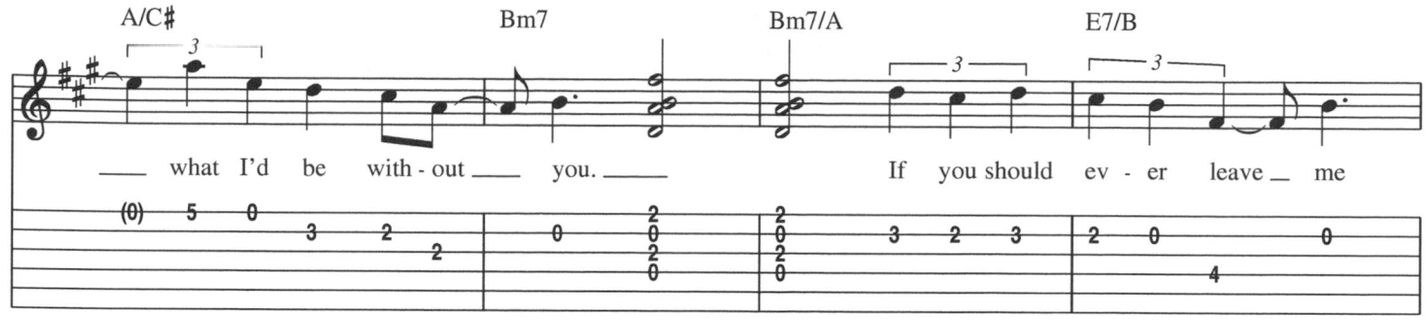

Additional Lyrics

2. If you should ever leave me,
   Well, life would still go on, believe me.
   The world could show nothing to me,
   So what good would living do me?
   God only knows what I'd be without you.

Fun, Fun, Fun

Words and Music by Brian Wilson and Mike Love

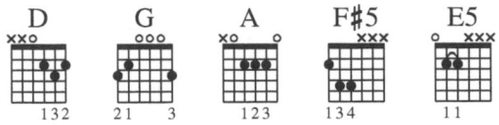

Strum Pattern: 2
Pick Pattern: 4

Verse

Moderately

mf

1. Well, she got her dad-dy's car and she cruised through the ham-bur-ger stand, now.
2., 3. *See additional lyrics*

Seems she for - got all a - bout the li - brar - y like she told her old man, now.

And with the ra - di - o blast - in' goes

Copyright © 1964 IRVING MUSIC, INC.
Copyright Renewed
All Rights Reserved Used by Permission

Additional Lyrics

2. Well, the girls can't stand her 'cause she walks, looks and drives like an ace, now.
   She makes the "Indy" Five Hundred look like a Roman chariot race, now.
   A lot of guys try to catch her, but she leads 'em on a wild goose chase, now.

3. Well, you knew all along that your dad was getting wise to you, now.
   And since he took your set of keys, you've been thinking that your fun is all through, now.
   But you can come along with me, 'cause we got a lot of things to do, now.

Good Vibrations

Words and Music by Brian Wilson and Mike Love

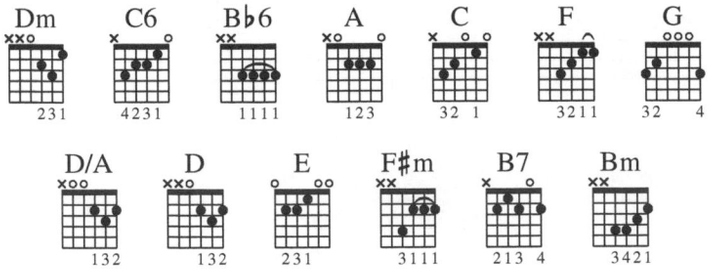

Strum Pattern: 4
Pick Pattern: 3

Verse

Moderately fast (♩♩ = ♩ ♪)

Dm C6

mf

1. I, _____ I love the col - or - ful clothes she wears, _____ and the
2. *See additional lyrics*

B♭6 A Dm

way the sun - light plays up - on __ her hair. _____ I _____

C6 B♭6

__ hear the sound of a gen - tle word _____ on the wind that lifts her per - fume through the air. _

Copyright © 1966 IRVING MUSIC, INC.
Copyright Renewed
All Rights Reserved Used by Permission

Chorus
A
C
F
I'm pick-in' up good vib - ra - tions. She's giv-in' me the
ex - cit - a - tions. I'm pick-in' up good vib - ra - tions. She's giv-in' me the ex - cit - a - tions.
(Good, bop, bop, good _ vib - ra - tions, bop, bop. Ex - cit - a -
G
I'm pick-in' up good vib - ra - tions. She's giv - in' me the ex - cit - a - tions.
- tions, bop, bop, good _ vib - ra - tions, bop, bop. Ex - cit - a -
A
1.
2.
I'm pick-in' up good vib - ra - tions. She's giv-in' me the ex - cit - a - tions. ex - cit - a - tions.
- tions, bop, bop. Good _ vib - ra - tions, bop, bop.) (Ex - cit - a...)
Interlude
A D/A A D/A A D/A A D/A A D/A
Mm,

A D/A A D/A A D/A D
mm. I don't know where, but she sends me there.

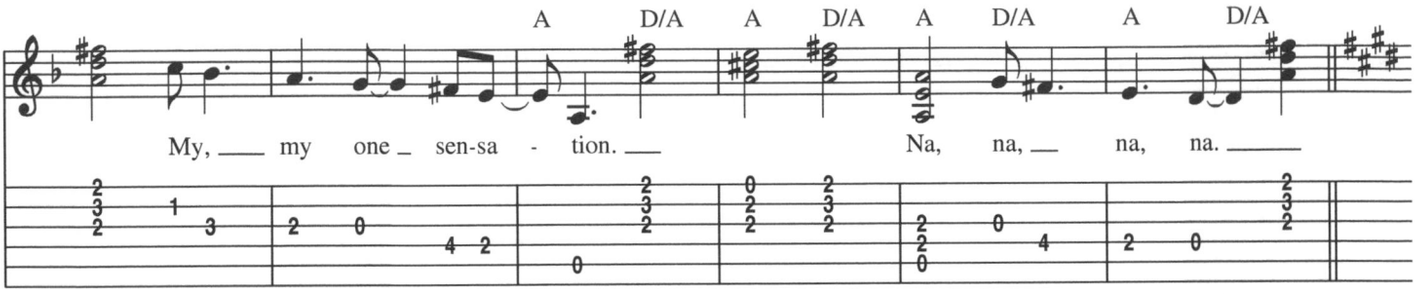
A D/A A D/A A D/A A D/A
My, my one sen-sa - tion. Na, na, na, na.

Pre-Chorus

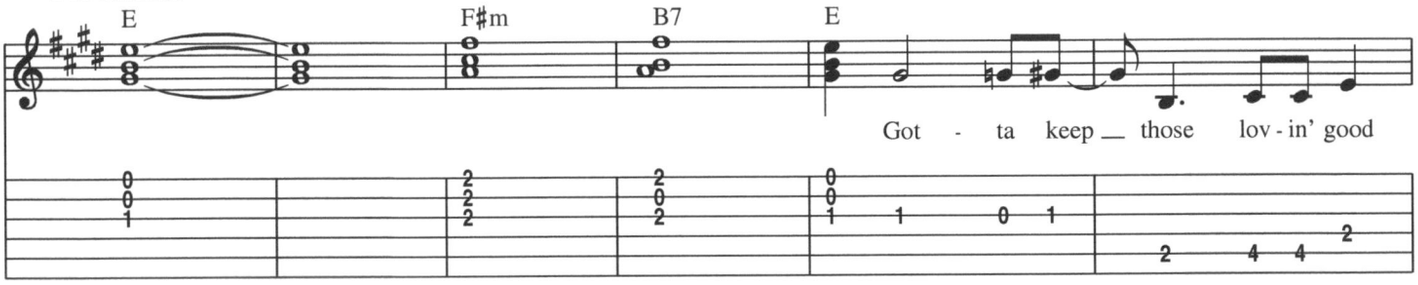
E F#m B7 E
Got - ta keep those lov - in' good

F#m B7 E
vib - ra - tions a - hap - p'nin' with her. Got - ta keep those lov - in' good

F#m B7 E Bm
vib - ra - tions a - hap - p'nin' with her. Ah.

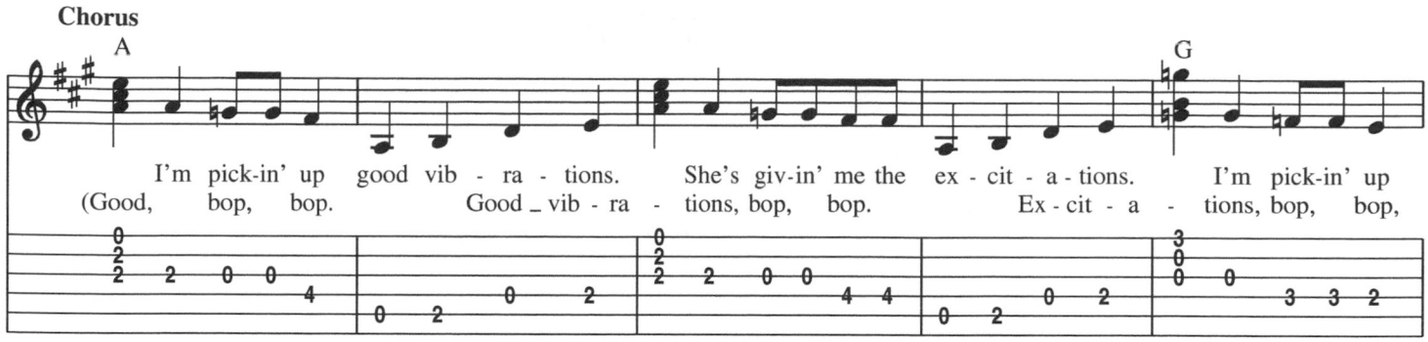

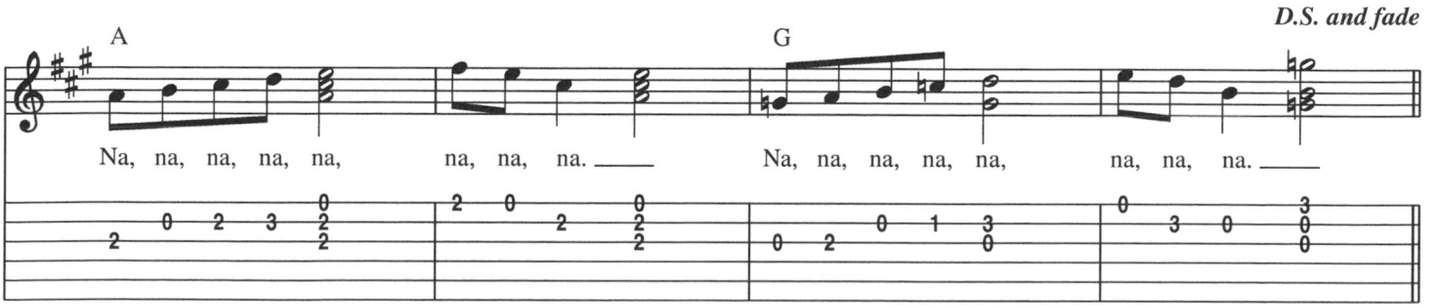

Additional Lyrics

2. Close my eyes, she's somehow closer now.
   Softly smile I know she must be kind.
   When I look in her eyes.
   She goes with me to a blossom room.

Help Me Rhonda

Words and Music by Brian Wilson and Mike Love

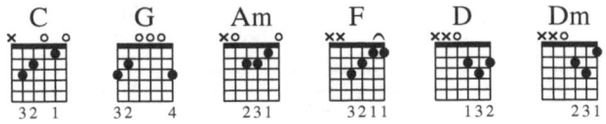

Strum Pattern: 2
Pick Pattern: 4

Intro
Moderate shuffle (♩♫ = ♩³♪)

C

mf

Verse

C G

1. Well, since she put me down I've been out do - in' in my head.
2. *See additional lyrics*

C

I come in late at night and in the

G C

morn - in' I just lay in bed. Well,

Copyright © 1965 IRVING MUSIC, INC.
Copyright Renewed
All Rights Reserved Used by Permission

Am
F
Rhon - da you look so fine, and I know it would - n't take much time,

D
C
Dm
N.C.
for you to help me Rhon - da, help me get her out of my heart.

Chorus
G
C
Help me Rhon - da, help, help me Rhon - da. Help me Rhon - da, help,

G
C
help me Rhon - da. Help me Rhon - da, help, help me Rhon - da. Help me Rhon - da, help,

F
Am
help me Rhon - da. Help me Rhon - da, help, help me Rhon - da. Help me Rhon - da, help,

Additional Lyrics

2. She was gonna be my wife and I was gonna be her man.
But she let another guy come between us and he shattered our plans.
Well, Rhonda you caught my eye, and I can give you lots of reasons why
You gotta help me Rhonda, help me get her out of my heart.

Little Deuce Coupe

Music by Brian Wilson
Words by Roger Christian

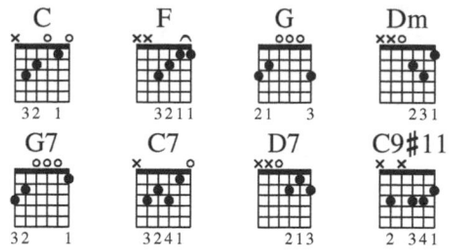

Strum Pattern: 2, 3
Pick Pattern: 3, 4

Verse

Moderate Rock (♩♩ = ♩♪)

C

1. Well, I'm not brag-gin', babe, so don't put me down, but I've got the fast-est set of
2. *See additional lyrics*

F

wheels in town. When some-thing pulls up to me, it don't e-ven try. And if it

C G Dm

had a set of wings, man, I know I could fly. She's my lit-tle deuce coupe,

Copyright © 1963 by Careers-BMG Music Publishing, Inc. and Irving Music, Inc.
Copyright Renewed
International Copyright Secured All Rights Reserved

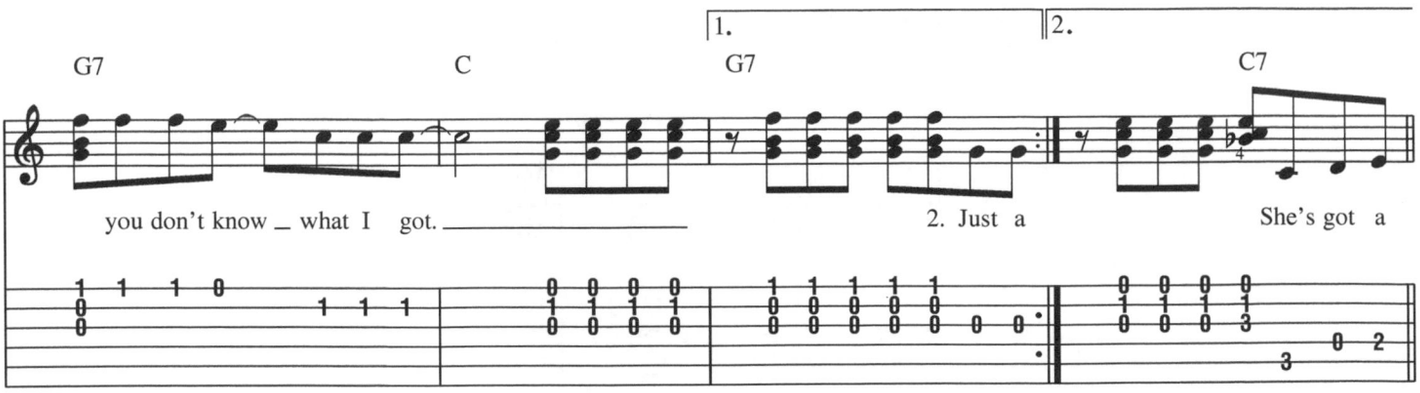
1.
2.
G7
C
G7
C7
you don't know _ what I got. _____
2. Just a
She's got a

Bridge
F
C
com - pe - ti - tion clutch, with four on the floor _ yeah, she purrs like a kit - ten till the

F
lake pipes roar. _ And if that ain't e - nough to make you flip your wig, _ there's

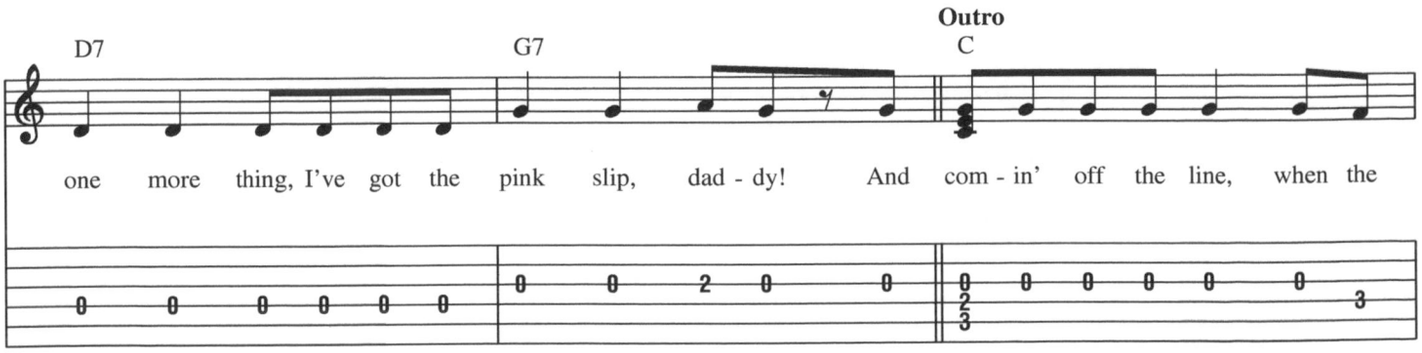
Outro
D7
G7
C
one more thing, I've got the pink slip, dad - dy! And com - in' off the line, when the

Additional Lyrics

2. Just a little deuce coupe with a flathead mill,
But she'll walk a Thunderbird like it's standin' still.
She's ported and relieved, and she's stroked and she's bored.
She'll do a hundred and forty with the top end floored.
She's my little deuce coupe,
You don't know what I got.

I Get Around

Words and Music by Brian Wilson and Mike Love

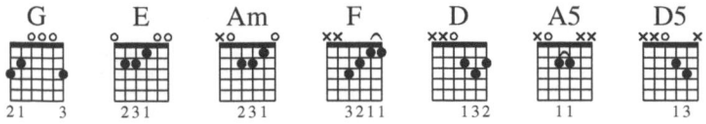

Strum Pattern: 2
Pick Pattern: 4

Intro
Moderately

N.C.(G) (E) (Am) (F) (D)

mf

Round, round, get a-round, I get a - round, yeah. Ooh, ooh. I get a -
(Get a-round, round, round, I get a - round.)

Chorus

G E

round, from town to town. I'm a real cool head,
(Get a-round, round, round, I get a-round. Get a-round, round, round, I get a - round.

Am F D

I'm mak-in' real good bread. 1. I'm get-tin'
Get a-round, round, round, I get a - round. Get a-round, round, round, I get a - round.)

Verse

A5 D5 A5 D5 A5 D5

bugged driv - in' up and down the same old strip. I got - ta find a new place where the
2. *See additional lyrics*

Copyright © 1964 IRVING MUSIC, INC.
Copyright Renewed
All Rights Reserved Used by Permission

Additional Lyrics

2. We always take my car 'cause it's never been beat.
And we've never missed yet with the girls we meet.
None of the guys go steady 'cause it wouldn't be right
To leave their best girl home on a Saturday night.

In My Room

Words and Music by Brian Wilson and Gary Usher

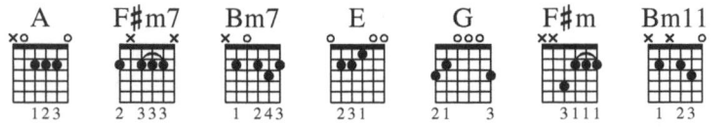

Strum Pattern: 8
Pick Pattern: 8

Intro

Moderately

A F♯m7 Bm7 E

mf

Verse

A

1. There's a world where
2. In this world I

I can go and tell my se - crets to. ___
lock out all my wor - ries and my fears. ___

G A F♯m7 Bm7 G

In ___ my room, ___

E A G

___ in ___ my room. ___

1. A

___

2. A

___

Copyright © 1964 IRVING MUSIC, INC.
Copyright Renewed
All Rights Reserved Used by Permission

Bridge
F♯m E F♯m E F♯m E A
Do my dream - ing and my schem - ing lie a - wake and pray.
F♯m E Bm7 Bm11 E
Do my cry - ing and my sigh - ing, laugh at yes - ter - day.
Verse
A G A F♯m7
3. Now it's dark and I'm a - lone, but I won't be a - fraid. In my
Bm7 G E
room, in my
Outro
Repeat and fade
A G A G A G A G
room. In my room, in my room. In my room, in my

Kokomo

from the Motion Picture COCKTAIL

Words and Music by Mike Love, Terry Melcher, John Phillips and Scott McKenzie

Strum Pattern: 3
Pick Pattern: 3

Intro

Moderately bright

N.C.

mf

A - ru - ba, Ja - mai - ca, oo ___ I wan - na take ya. Ber - mu - da, Ba - ha - ma, come_

___ on, pret - ty ma - ma. Key Lar - go, Mon - te - go, ba - by why don't we go, Ja -

Verse

C Cmaj7 Gm7

mai - ca. 1. Off the Flor - i - da Keys ___ there's a place called

F Fm C D7

Ko - ko - mo. ___ That's where you want to go ___ to get a - way from it all. ___

© 1988 Touchstone Pictures Music & Songs, Inc., Buena Vista Music Company, Clair Audient Publishing,
Daywin Music, Inc., Honest John Music and Phillips-Tucker Music
Aministered 100% by Touchstone Pictures Music & Songs, Inc. and Buena Vista Music Company
All Rights Reserved Used by Permission

Verse
G7
C
Cmaj7
Gm7
2. Bod-ies in the sand, trop - i - cal drink melt-ing
4. See additional lyrics
F
Fm
C
in your hand. We'll be fall - ing in love to the rhy - thm of a
D7
G7
Chorus
C
steel drum band down in Ko - ko - mo. A - ru - ba, Ja - mai - ca, oo
F
I wan - na take you to Ber - mu - da, Ba - ha - ma, come on, pret - ty ma - ma. Key
C
F
Lar - go, Mon - te - go, oo I wan - na take you down to Ko - ko - mo, we'll

Fm C Am Dm
get there fast and then we'll take it slow. That's where we wan - na go,
G7 C
way down in Ko - ko - mo.
Mar - tin - ique, that Mon-ser - rat mys-tique.
Port Au Prince, I wan-na catch a glimpse.
Verse
C
3. We'll put out to sea,
5. Ev - 'ry-bod - y knows,
Cmaj7 Gm7 F
and we'll per - fect our chem - is - try.
a lit - tle place like Ko - ko - mo.
1.
Fm
By and by we'll de - fy
C D7 G7
a lit - tle bit of grav - i - ty.
2.
Fm
Now if you
C D7 G7
wan - na go to get a - way from it all,
go down to Ko - ko - mo. A -

Additional Lyrics

4. Afternoon delight,
   Cocktails and moonlit nights.
   That dreamy look in your eye
   Gives me a tropical contact high,
   Way down in Kokomo.

Shut Down

Words by Roger Christian
Music by Brian Wilson

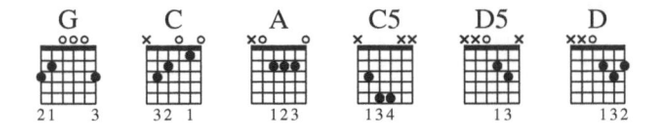

Strum Pattern: 2, 6
Pick Pattern: 3, 4

Intro
Bright Rock

N.C.(A) (C5) (D5) G

mf

Tach it up, tach it up, bud - dy, gon - na shut you down.

TAB

0 0 0 0 0 0 | 4 4 4 4 3 3 3 | 3 3 3 3 3

Verse

G

1. It hap - pened on the strip where the road is wide,
2., 3. *See additional lyrics*

3 3 3 3 3 0 | 0 0 1 0 3 1 0 | 1 0 0 3

C

two cool shorts stand - in' side by side. Yeah, my fuel - in - ject - ed Sting - ray and a

0 0 3 1 0 | 1 0 0 3 3 | 1 1 1 1 1 1 0 3 0

Copyright © 1963 IRVING MUSIC, INC.
Copyright Renewed and Assigned to IRVING MUSIC, INC. and CAREERS-BMG MUSIC PUBLISHING, INC. for the USA
All Rights Reserved Used by Permission

G
Four - thir - teen, rev - in' up our en - gines and it sounds real mean.

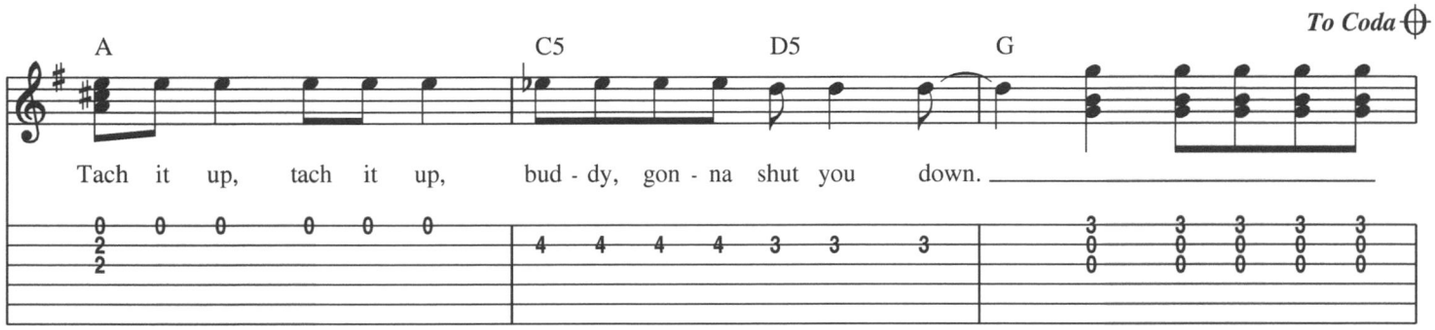
To Coda
A
C5
D5
G
Tach it up, tach it up, bud - dy, gon - na shut you down.

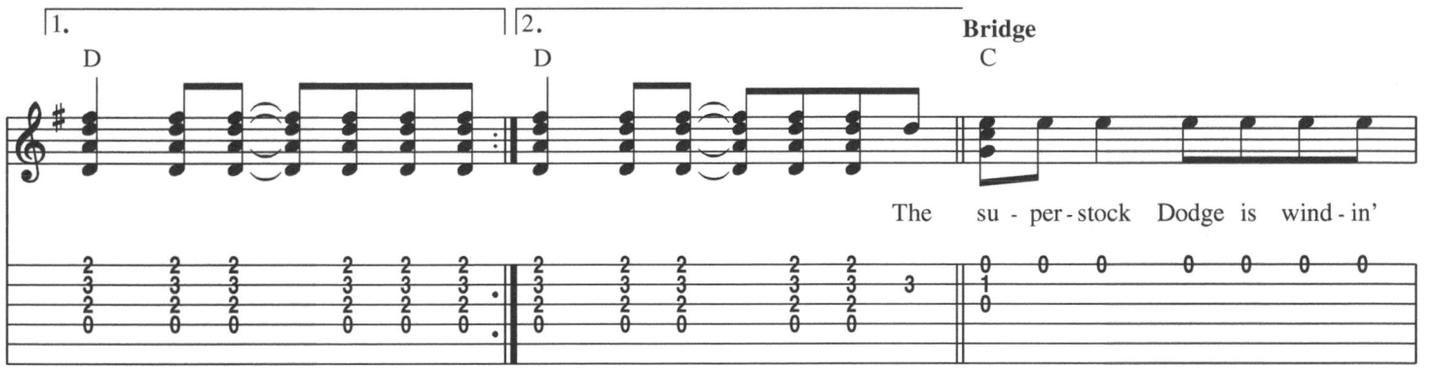
1.
2.
Bridge
D
D
C
The su - per - stock Dodge is wind - in'

G
out in low, but my fuel - in - ject - ed Sting-ray's real - ly start - in' to go. To

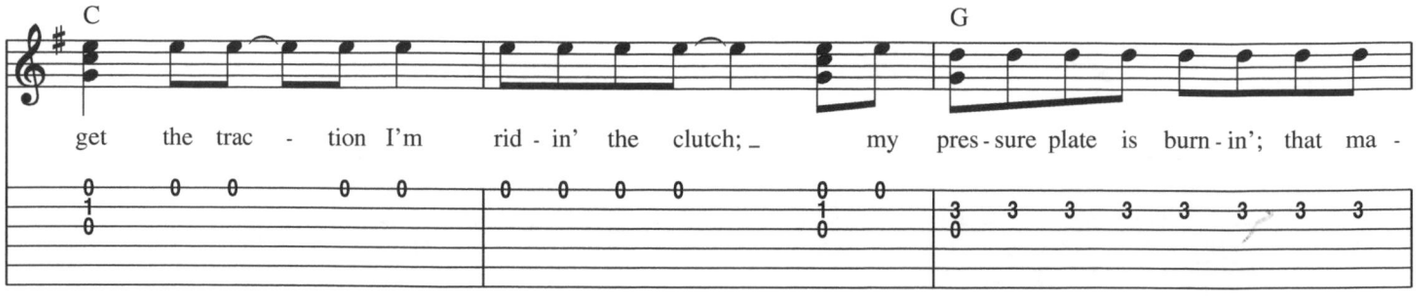

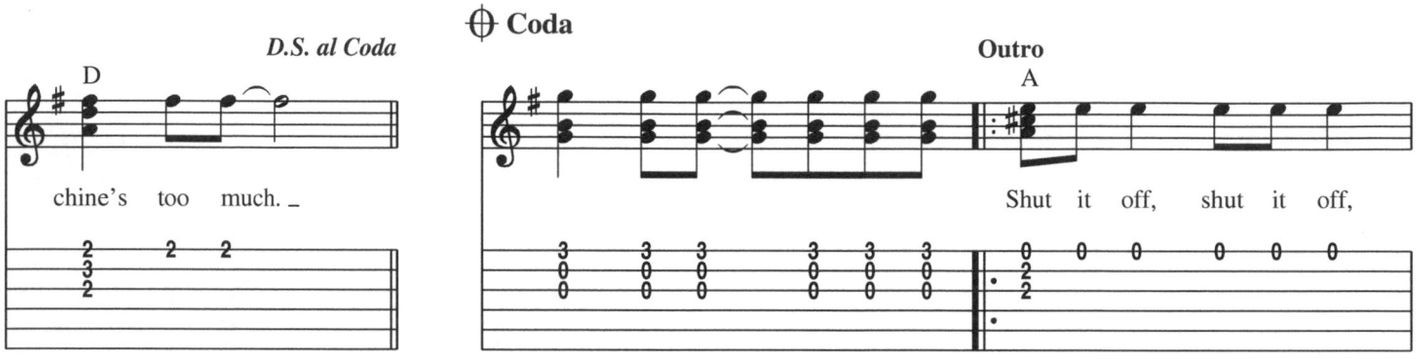

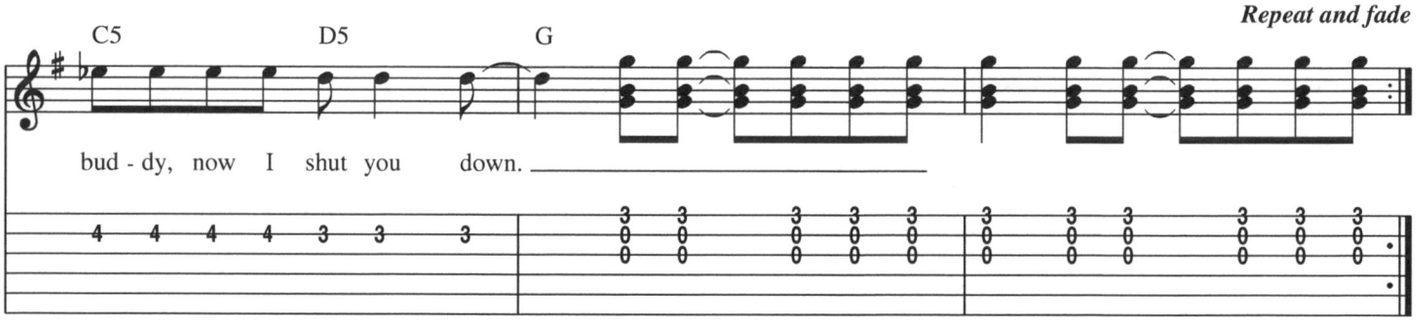

Additional Lyrics

2. Declinin' numbers at an even rate,
   At the count of one we both accelerate.
   My Stingray is light, the slicks are startin' to spin,
   But the Four-thirteen's really diggin' in.
   Gotta be cool now, power shift, here we go.

3. Pedal's to the floor, hear his dual quads drive,
   And now the Four-thirteen's lead is startin' to shrink.
   He's hot with ram induction, but it's understood.
   I got a fuel-injected engine sittin' under my hood.
   Shut it off, shut if off, buddy, now I shut you down.

Sloop John B

Words and Music by Brian Wilson

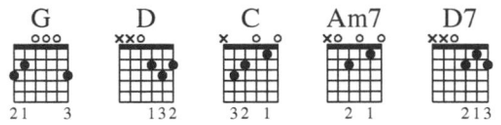

Strum Pattern: 6
Pick Pattern: 4

Verse

Moderately

G

mf

1. We come out in the Sloop John B, my grand - fa - ther and

2., 3. *See additional lyrics*

me, a - round Nas - sau town we ____ do roam.

D

Drink - ing all night; got in - to a

G

Copyright © 1966 New Executive Music
Copyright Renewed
International Copyright Secured All Rights Reserved

C
Am7
G
D7
fight.
Well, I feel so broke _ up,
I wan - na go

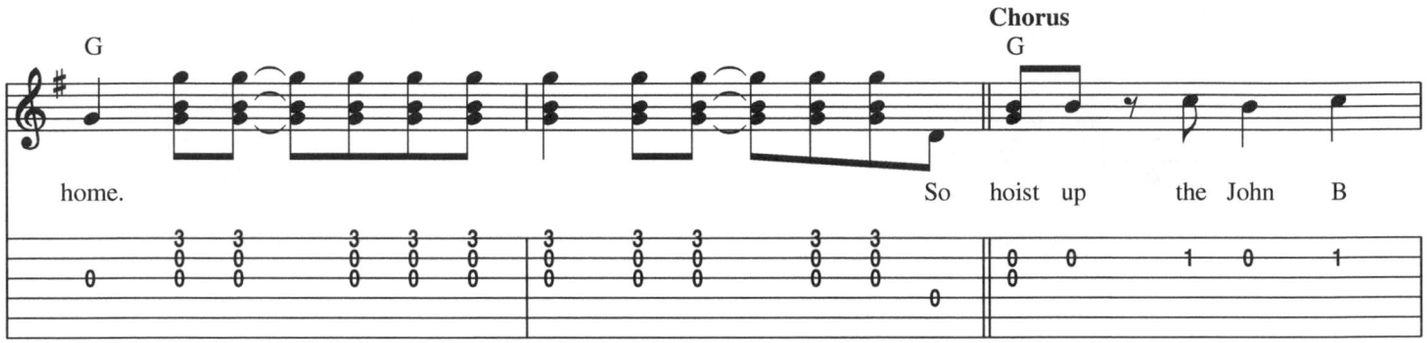
G
Chorus
G
home.
So hoist up the John B

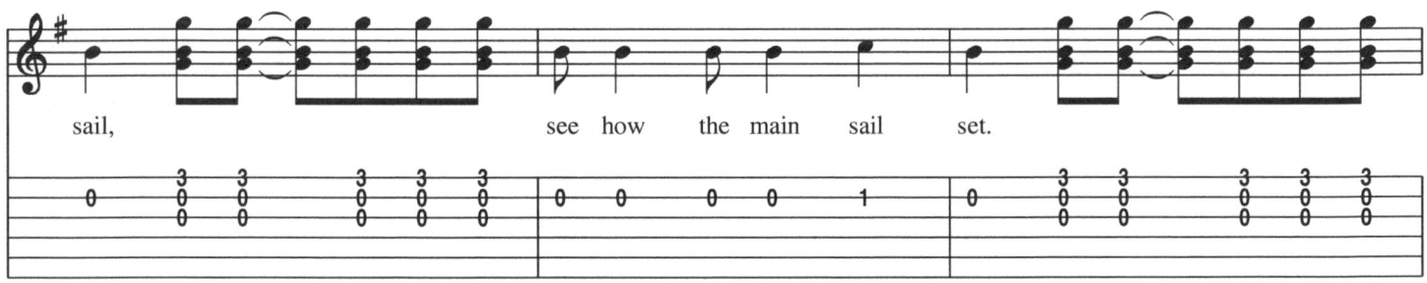
sail,
see how the main sail set.

D
Call for the Cap - tain a - shore, let ___ me go home. _____

Additional Lyrics

2. So first mate, he got drunk,
   He broke in the Captain's trunk.
   The constable had to come and take him away.
   Sheriff John Stone,
   Why don't you leave me alone?
   Well, I feel so broke up, I wanna go home.

3. The poor cook, he got the fits,
   He threw away all my grits
   And then he took and he ate up all of my corn.
   Let me go home.
   Why don't they let me go home?
   This is the worst trip I've ever been on.

Surfer Girl

Words and Music by Brian Wilson

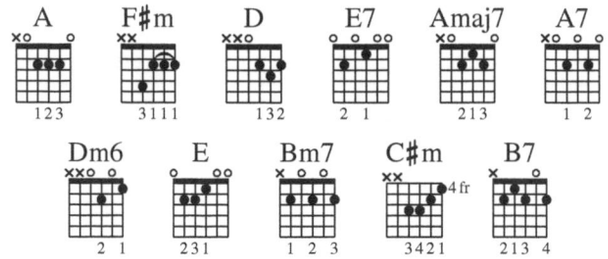

Strum Pattern: 8
Pick Pattern: 8

Verse

Moderately

A F♯m D E7 Amaj7 A7 D Dm6 A F♯m

mf

1. Lit - tle surf - er, lit - tle one, made my heart come all un - done. Do you love me,
2. *See additional lyrics*

D E7 A F♯m D E7

do you surf - er girl?

2. A D E E7

girl?

Bridge

D E7

We could ride

A Bm7 E7 A

the surf to - geth - er while our love would grow.

© Copyright 1962 by Guild Music Company
Copyright Renewed
International Copyright Secured All Rights Reserved

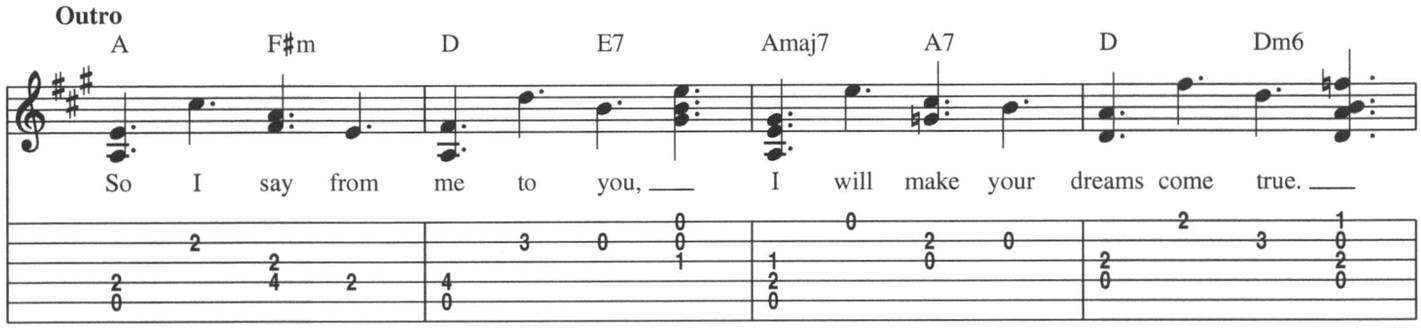

Additional Lyrics

2. I have watched you on the shore,
Standing by the ocean's roar.
Do you love me, do you surfer girl?

Surfin'

Words and Music by Brian Wilson and Mike Love

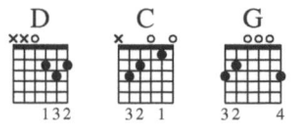

Strum Pattern: 2
Pick Pattern: 4

Intro
Moderately

D C D

mf

Surf - in' is the on - ly life, the on - ly way for me, now surf,

C G **Verse** G

surf with me. 1. I got up this morn - in', turned _
2., 3. *See additional lyrics*

on my ra - di - o, I was check - in' out the surf - in' scene to see if I would go. And when the

C D

D. J. tells me that the surf - in' is fine, that's when I know my ba - by and I will

© Copyright 1962 by Guild Music Company
Copyright Renewed
International Copyright Secured All Rights Reserved

Additional Lyrics

2. From the early mornin' to the middle of the night,
   Any time the surf is up, the time is right.
   And when the surf is down, to take its place,
   We'll do the surfer stomp; it's the latest dance craze.

3. Now the dawn is breakin' and we really gotta go.
   But we'll be back here very soon; that you better know.
   Yeah, my surfer knots are risin' and my board is losin' wax,
   But that won't stop me, baby, 'cause you know I'm comin' back.

Surfin' Safari

Words and Music by Brian Wilson and Mike Love

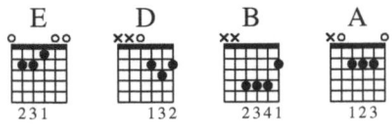

Strum Pattern: 2
Pick Pattern: 4

Intro-Chorus
Moderately

E N.C. D N.C. B N.C. B N.C.

mf

Let's go surf - in' now, ev - 'ry - bod - y's learn - in' how, come on a sa - fa - ri with me.

Verse

E A D

(Come on a sa - fa - ri with

1. Ear - ly in the morn-in' we'll be start - in' out, some me.)

2., 4. *See additional lyrics*

3. *Instrumental*

(2)

E A D

hon-eys will be com-in' a - long. We're load-in' up our wood-y with the boards in - side and

Chorus

E A A

head-in' out sing-in' our song. Come on, ba - by, wait and see, yes,

© Copyright 1962 by Guild Music Company
Copyright Renewed
International Copyright Secured All Rights Reserved

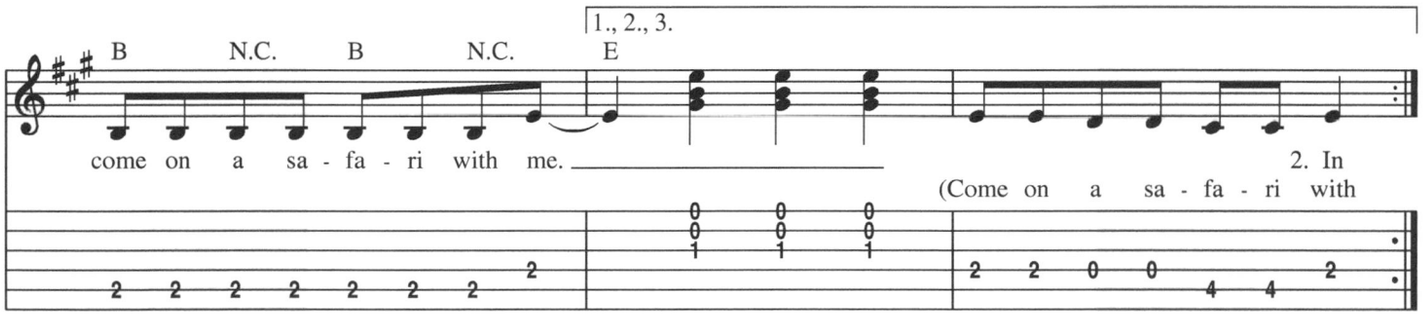

Additional Lyrics

2. In Huntington and Malibu they're shootin' the pier,
In Rincon, they're walkin' the nose.
We're goin' on safari to the islands this year,
So if you're comin', get ready to go.

4. They're anglin' in Laguna and Cerro Azul,
They're kickin' out in Dohini too.
I'll tell you surfin's runnin' wild, it's gettin' bigger ev'ry day
From Hawaii to the shores of Peru.

Wouldn't It Be Nice

Words and Music by Brian Wilson, Tony Asher and Mike Love

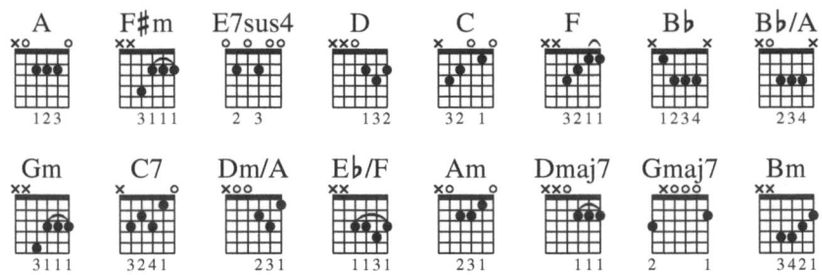

Strum Pattern: 2
Pick Pattern: 4

Intro

Moderately (♩♩ = ♩ ♪)

A F♯m E7sus4 D A F♯m

mf

TAB

Verse

C F

1. Would - n't it be nice if we were old - er? Then _ we would-n't

2. *See additional lyrics*

B♭ B♭/A Gm C7 F

have to wait so ___ long. _____ And would-n't it be nice to live to - geth -

Copyright © 1966 IRVING MUSIC, INC.
Copyright Renewed
All Rights Reserved Used by Permission

B♭
B♭/A
Gm
C7
- er in the kind of world where we'd be - long?

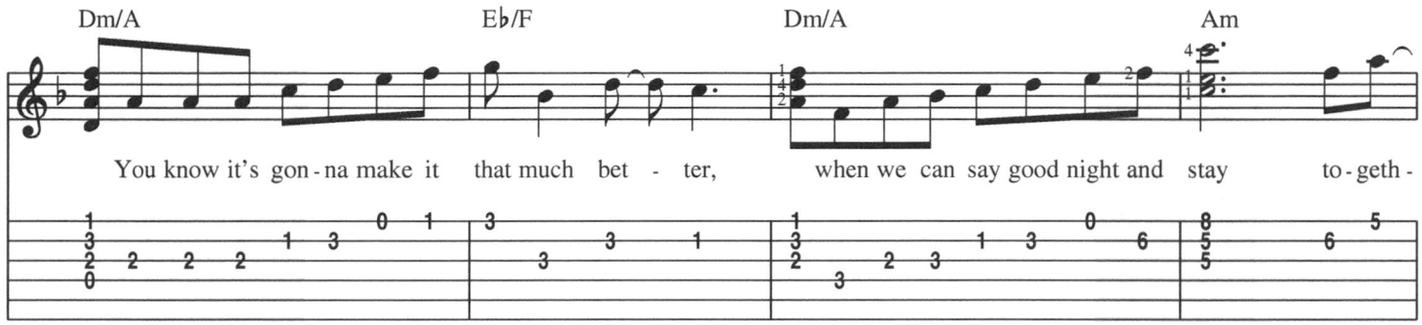
Dm/A
E♭/F
Dm/A
Am
You know it's gon - na make it that much bet - ter, when we can say good night and stay to - geth -

Gm
1.
C7
2.
C7
F
- er. 2. Would - n't it be Would - n't it be nice?

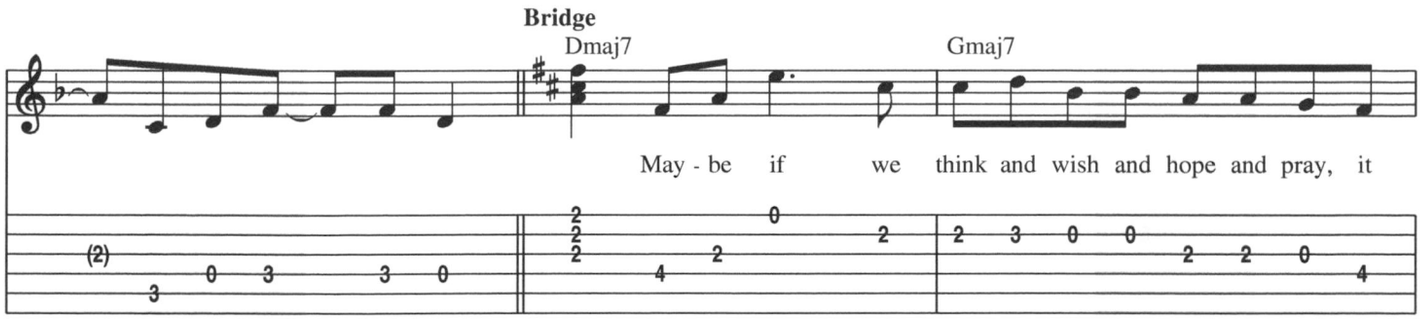
Bridge
Dmaj7
Gmaj7
May - be if we think and wish and hope and pray, it

F♯m
Bm
Dmaj7
Gmaj7
might come true. (Run, run, wee.) Ba - by then there would-n't be a sin - gle thing we

F♯m
Bm
F♯m
could - n't do. A we could be mar - ried. A we could be mar -

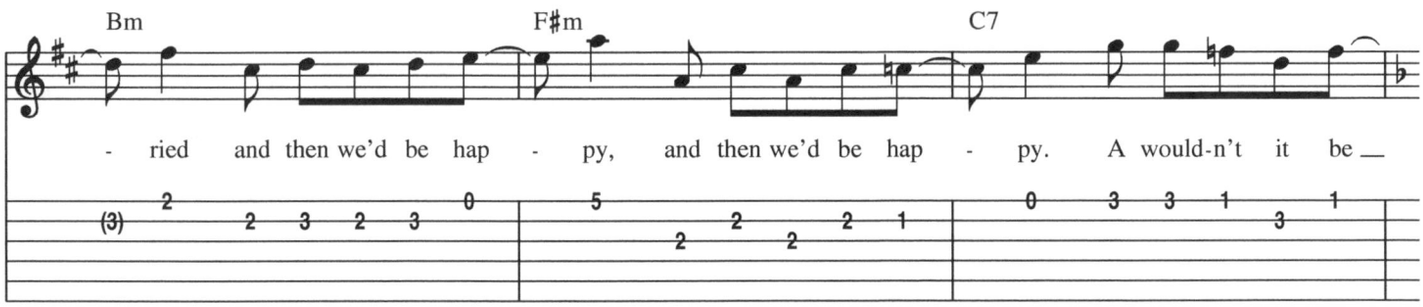
Bm
F♯m
C7
- ried and then we'd be hap - py, and then we'd be hap - py. A would-n't it be

F
nice? (Ba, ba, ba. Be, doo, be, doo. Ba, ba, ba, ba,

Additional Lyrics

2. Wouldn't it be nice if we could wake up
In the morning when the day is new.
And after havin' spent the day together,
Hold each other close the whole night through.
Well, happy times together, we'd be spending.
I wish that ev'ry kiss was never ending.
Wouldn't it be nice?

Surfin' U.S.A.

Words and Music by Chuck Berry

Copyright © 1958, 1963 (Renewed) by Arc Music Corporation (BMI) and Isalee Music Inc. (BMI)
International Copyright Secured All Rights Reserved
Used by Permission

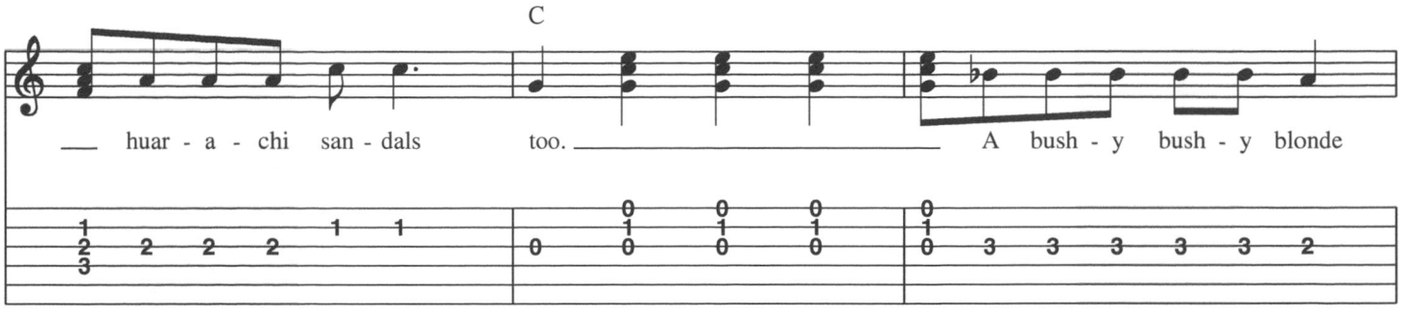
C
huar - a - chi san - dals too. A bush - y bush - y blonde

G7
C
hair - do, surf - in' U. S. A.

Verse

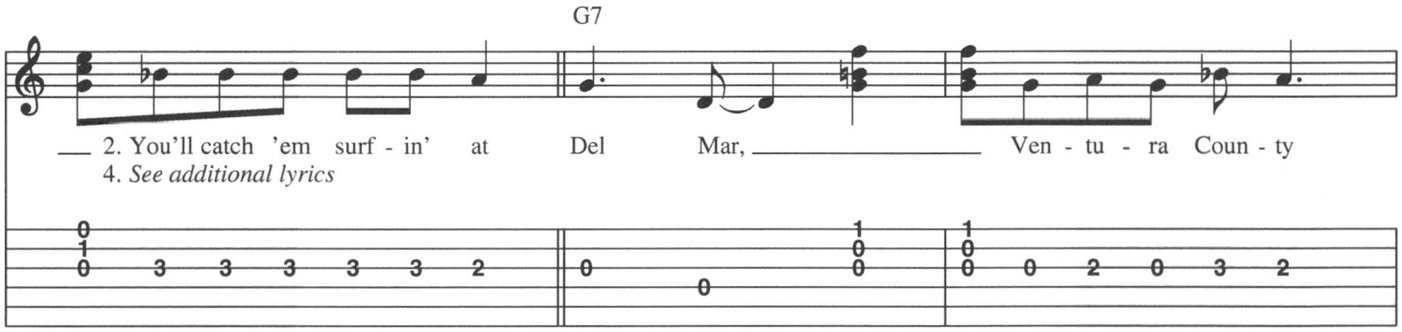
G7
2. You'll catch 'em surf - in' at Del Mar, Ven - tu - ra Coun - ty
4. *See additional lyrics*

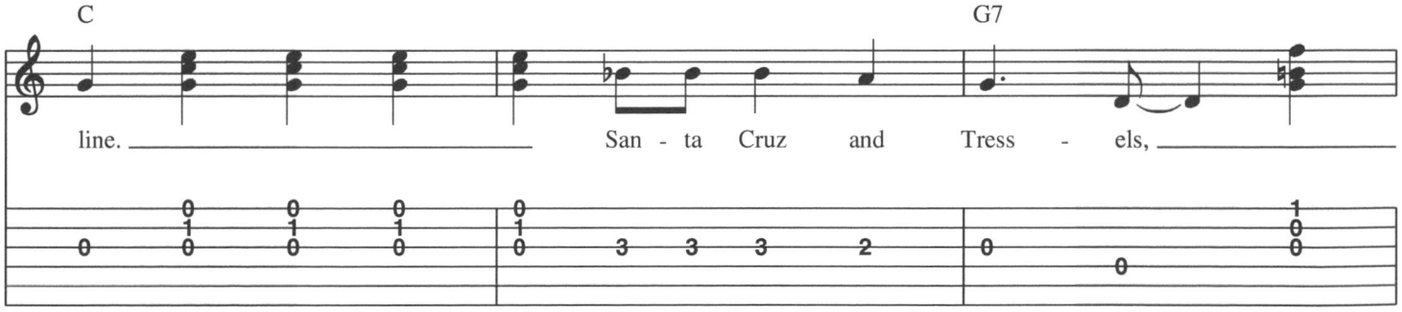
C
G7
line. San - ta Cruz and Tress - els,

C
Aus - tra - lia's Nar - a - bine. All o - ver Man -

Additional Lyrics

3. We'll all be plannin' out a route
Were gonna take real soon.
We're waxin' down our surfboards,
We can't wait for June.
We'll all be gone for the summer,
We're on safari to stay.
Tell the teacher we're surfin',
Surfin' U.S.A.

4. At Haggarty's and Swami's
Pacific Palisades.
San Onfre and Sunset,
Redondo Beach L.A.
All over La Jolla,
at Waiamea Bay.
Ev'rybody's gone surfin',
Surfin' U.S.A.